Good Day
Start
With Gratitude

>>> ———————— <<<

This Journal Belongs To :

_____

_____

Date:

Quote Of The Day

_____

_____

Today I am truly grateful for...

_____

_____

_____

_____

Here's what would make today great...

_____

_____

_____

_____

I am...

_____

_____

Some amazing things that happened today...

_____

_____

Some amazing things that happened today...

_____

_____

What could I have done to make today even better?

_____

_____

Date: _____

Quote Of The Day

_____
_____
_____

Today I am truly grateful for...

_____
_____
_____
_____
_____

Here's what would make today great...

_____
_____
_____
_____
_____

I am...

_____
_____
_____

Some amazing things that happened today...

_____
_____

Some amazing things that happened today...

_____
_____

What could I have done to make today even better?

_____
_____

Date: ☀

Quote Of The Day

_____

_____

Today I am truly grateful for...

_____

_____

_____

_____

Here's what would make today great...

_____

_____

_____

_____

I am...

_____

_____

Some amazing things that happened today...

_____

Some amazing things that happened today...   ✦ ✦ 🌙

_____

_____

What could I have done to make today even better?

_____

Date: ....

Quote Of The Day

_____

_____

Today I am truly grateful for...

_____

_____

_____

_____

Here's what would make today great...

_____

_____

_____

_____

I am...

_____

_____

_____

Some amazing things that happened today...

_____

_____

Some amazing things that happened today...

_____

_____

What could I have done to make today even better?

_____

_____

Date:

Quote Of The Day

Today I am truly grateful for...

Here's what would make today great...

I am...

Some amazing things that happened today...

Some amazing things that happened today...

What could I have done to make today even better?

ate:

Note Of The Day

_____
_____

Today I am truly grateful for...

_____
_____
_____
_____

Here's what would make today great...

_____
_____
_____
_____

I am...

_____
_____

Some amazing things that happened today...

_____

Some amazing things that happened today...

_____
_____

What could I have done to make today even better?

_____
_____

Date:

Quote Of The Day

_____

_____

_____

Today I am truly grateful for...

_____

_____

_____

_____

Here's what would make today great...

_____

_____

_____

_____

I am...

_____

_____

_____

Some amazing things that happened today...

_____

_____

Some amazing things that happened today...

_____

_____

What could I have done to make today even better?

_____

_____

Date:

Quote Of The Day

_____
_____

Today I am truly grateful for...

_____
_____
_____
_____

Here's what would make today great...

_____
_____
_____
_____

I am...

_____
_____

Some amazing things that happened today...

_____

Some amazing things that happened today...

_____
_____

What could I have done to make today even better?

_____
_____

Date: _____

Quote Of The Day

_____

_____

_____

Today I am truly grateful for...

_____

_____

_____

_____

_____

Here's what would make today great...

_____

_____

_____

_____

_____

I am...

_____

_____

_____

Some amazing things that happened today...

_____

_____

Some amazing things that happened today...

_____

_____

What could I have done to make today even better?

_____

_____

Date: _____

☀

Quote Of The Day
_____
_____

Today I am truly grateful for...
_____
_____
_____
_____

Here's what would make today great...
_____
_____
_____
_____

I am...
_____
_____
_____

Some amazing things that happened today...
_____
_____

Some amazing things that happened today...
_____
_____

What could I have done to make today even better?
_____
_____

Date:

Quote Of The Day

_____

_____

_____

Today I am truly grateful for...

_____

_____

_____

_____

_____

Here's what would make today great...

_____

_____

_____

_____

_____

I am...

_____

_____

_____

Some amazing things that happened today...

_____

_____

Some amazing things that happened today...

_____

_____

_____

What could I have done to make today even better?

_____

_____

ate: _____

☀

ote Of The Day

_____

_____

day I am truly grateful for...

_____

_____

_____

_____

_____

re's what would make today great...

_____

_____

_____

_____

am...

_____

_____

me amazing things that happened today...

_____

me amazing things that happened today...

_____

_____

nat could I have done to make today even better?

_____

_____

Date:

Quote Of The Day

_____

_____

Today I am truly grateful for...

_____

_____

_____

_____

Here's what would make today great...

_____

_____

_____

_____

I am...

_____

_____

Some amazing things that happened today...

_____

_____

Some amazing things that happened today...

_____

_____

What could I have done to make today even better?

_____

_____

Date: _____

Quote Of The Day
_____
_____
_____

Today I am truly grateful for...
_____
_____
_____
_____
_____

Here's what would make today great...
_____
_____
_____
_____

I am...
_____
_____
_____

Some amazing things that happened today...
_____
_____

Some amazing things that happened today...
_____
_____

What could I have done to make today even better?
_____
_____

Date: ☼

Quote Of The Day

_____

_____

_____

Today I am truly grateful for...

_____

_____

_____

_____

_____

Here's what would make today great...

_____

_____

_____

_____

_____

I am...

_____

_____

_____

Some amazing things that happened today...

_____

_____

Some amazing things that happened today... ✨ ✨ 🌙

_____

_____

What could I have done to make today even better?

_____

_____

Date: _____

☀

Quote Of The Day
_____
_____

Today I am truly grateful for...
_____
_____
_____
_____

Here's what would make today great...
_____
_____
_____
_____

I am...
_____
_____

Some amazing things that happened today...
_____

Some amazing things that happened today...
_____

What could I have done to make today even better?
_____
_____

Date:

Quote Of The Day

Today I am truly grateful for...

Here's what would make today great...

I am...

Some amazing things that happened today...

Some amazing things that happened today...

What could I have done to make today even better?

ate: ....

Note Of The Day

_____

_____

Today I am truly grateful for...

_____

_____

_____

_____

Here's what would make today great...

_____

_____

_____

_____

I am...

_____

_____

Some amazing things that happened today...

_____

Some amazing things that happened today...

_____

What could I have done to make today even better?

_____

Date: _____

Quote Of The Day

_____

_____

Today I am truly grateful for...

_____

_____

_____

_____

Here's what would make today great...

_____

_____

_____

_____

I am...

_____

_____

Some amazing things that happened today...

_____

_____

Some amazing things that happened today...

_____

_____

What could I have done to make today even better?

_____

Date:

Quote Of The Day

_____

_____

Today I am truly grateful for...

_____

_____

_____

_____

Here's what would make today great...

_____

_____

_____

_____

I am...

_____

_____

Some amazing things that happened today...

_____

_____

Some amazing things that happened today...

_____

_____

What could I have done to make today even better?

_____

_____

Date: _____

Quote Of The Day

_____
_____

Today I am truly grateful for...

_____
_____
_____
_____
_____

Here's what would make today great...

_____
_____
_____
_____
_____

I am...

_____
_____
_____

Some amazing things that happened today...

_____
_____

Some amazing things that happened today...

_____
_____
_____

What could I have done to make today even better?

_____
_____

Date:

Quote Of The Day
_____
_____

Today I am truly grateful for...
_____
_____
_____
_____

Here's what would make today great...
_____
_____
_____
_____
_____

I am...
_____
_____
_____

Some amazing things that happened today...
_____
_____

Some amazing things that happened today...
_____
_____

What could I have done to make today even better?
_____
_____

Date:

Quote Of The Day

_____

Today I am truly grateful for...

_____
_____
_____
_____

Here's what would make today great...

_____
_____
_____
_____

I am...

_____
_____

Some amazing things that happened today...

_____
_____

Some amazing things that happened today...

_____
_____

What could I have done to make today even better?

_____
_____

ate: _____

Note Of The Day

_____
_____
_____

day I am truly grateful for...

_____
_____
_____
_____
_____

re's what would make today great...

_____
_____
_____
_____

am...

_____
_____
_____

me amazing things that happened today...

_____

ome amazing things that happened today...

_____
_____

hat could I have done to make today even better?

_____
_____

Date: ☀

Quote Of The Day
_____
_____

Today I am truly grateful for...
_____
_____
_____
_____
_____

Here's what would make today great...
_____
_____
_____
_____
_____

I am...
_____
_____

Some amazing things that happened today...
_____
_____

Some amazing things that happened today... ✧ ✧ ☾
_____
_____

What could I have done to make today even better?
_____
_____

Date: _____

_____

_____

Today I am truly grateful for...

_____

_____

_____

_____

Here's what would make today great...

_____

_____

_____

_____

I am...

_____

_____

_____

Some amazing things that happened today...

_____

_____

Some amazing things that happened today...

_____

_____

What could I have done to make today even better?

_____

_____

Date: _____

Quote Of The Day

_____
_____

Today I am truly grateful for...

_____
_____
_____
_____

Here's what would make today great...

_____
_____
_____
_____

I am...

_____
_____
_____

Some amazing things that happened today...

_____
_____

Some amazing things that happened today...

_____
_____

What could I have done to make today even better?

_____
_____

Date: _____

☀

Quote Of The Day
_____
_____

Today I am truly grateful for...
_____
_____
_____
_____

Here's what would make today great...
_____
_____
_____
_____

I am...
_____
_____
_____

Some amazing things that happened today...
_____
_____

Some amazing things that happened today...

☽

_____
_____

What could I have done to make today even better?
_____
_____

Date:

Quote Of The Day

_____

Today I am truly grateful for...

_____

_____

_____

_____

Here's what would make today great...

_____

_____

_____

_____

I am...

_____

_____

Some amazing things that happened today...

_____

_____

Some amazing things that happened today...

_____

_____

What could I have done to make today even better?

_____

_____

Date: ☀

Quote Of The Day
_____
_____

Today I am truly grateful for...
_____
_____
_____
_____
_____

Here's what would make today great...
_____
_____
_____
_____
_____

I am...
_____
_____
_____

Some amazing things that happened today...
_____
_____

Some amazing things that happened today...
_____
_____

What could I have done to make today even better?
_____
_____

Date: _____

Quote Of The Day

_____
_____
_____

Today I am truly grateful for...

_____
_____
_____
_____
_____

Here's what would make today great...

_____
_____
_____
_____
_____

I am...

_____
_____
_____

Some amazing things that happened today...

_____
_____

Some amazing things that happened today...

_____
_____

What could I have done to make today even better?

_____
_____

Date: _____

Quote Of The Day

_____
_____
_____

Today I am truly grateful for...

_____
_____
_____
_____
_____

Here's what would make today great...

_____
_____
_____
_____
_____

I am...

_____
_____
_____

Some amazing things that happened today...

_____
_____

Some amazing things that happened today...

_____
_____
_____

What could I have done to make today even better?

_____
_____

Date: _____

Quote Of The Day

_____

_____

Today I am truly grateful for...

_____

_____

_____

_____

Here's what would make today great...

_____

_____

_____

_____

I am...

_____

_____

Some amazing things that happened today...

_____

Some amazing things that happened today...

_____

_____

What could I have done to make today even better?

_____

_____

ate: _____

☀

uote Of The Day

_____
_____

day I am truly grateful for...

_____
_____
_____
_____

ere's what would make today great...

_____
_____
_____
_____

am...

_____
_____
_____

me amazing things that happened today...

_____
_____

ome amazing things that happened today...

_____
_____

hat could I have done to make today even better?

_____
_____

Date:

Quote Of The Day

_____

_____

Today I am truly grateful for...

_____

_____

_____

_____

_____

Here's what would make today great...

_____

_____

_____

_____

_____

I am...

_____

_____

_____

Some amazing things that happened today...

_____

_____

Some amazing things that happened today...

_____

_____

What could I have done to make today even better?

_____

_____

ate: ‥‥‥‥‥‥‥‥

☀

ote Of The Day

_____
_____
_____

day I am truly grateful for...

_____
_____
_____
_____
_____

re's what would make today great...

_____
_____
_____
_____

am...

_____
_____
_____

me amazing things that happened today...

_____
_____

ome amazing things that happened today...

☆ ☆ ☽

_____
_____

nat could I have done to make today even better?

_____
_____

Date:

Quote Of The Day

_____

_____

Today I am truly grateful for...

_____

_____

_____

_____

Here's what would make today great...

_____

_____

_____

_____

I am...

_____

_____

Some amazing things that happened today...

_____

_____

Some amazing things that happened today...

_____

_____

What could I have done to make today even better?

_____

_____

Date:

Quote Of The Day

_____

_____

_____

Today I am truly grateful for...

_____

_____

_____

_____

Here's what would make today great...

_____

_____

_____

_____

I am...

_____

_____

_____

Some amazing things that happened today...

_____

_____

Some amazing things that happened today...

_____

_____

_____

What could I have done to make today even better?

_____

_____

Date: _____

Quote Of The Day

_____

_____

Today I am truly grateful for...

_____

_____

_____

_____

Here's what would make today great...

_____

_____

_____

_____

I am...

_____

_____

Some amazing things that happened today...

_____

_____

Some amazing things that happened today...

_____

_____

What could I have done to make today even better?

_____

_____

ate:

Quote Of The Day
_____
_____

Today I am truly grateful for...
_____
_____
_____
_____

Here's what would make today great...
_____
_____
_____
_____

I am...
_____
_____

Some amazing things that happened today...
_____
_____

Some amazing things that happened today...
_____
_____

What could I have done to make today even better?
_____
_____

Date: _____

Quote Of The Day

_____

_____

_____

Today I am truly grateful for...

_____

_____

_____

_____

_____

Here's what would make today great...

_____

_____

_____

_____

_____

I am...

_____

_____

_____

Some amazing things that happened today...

_____

_____

Some amazing things that happened today...

_____

_____

_____

What could I have done to make today even better?

_____

_____

Date: _____

☼

Note Of The Day
_____
_____
_____

Today I am truly grateful for...
_____
_____
_____
_____
_____

Here's what would make today great...
_____
_____
_____
_____
_____

I am...
_____
_____
_____

Some amazing things that happened today...
_____
_____

Some amazing things that happened today...
_____

What could I have done to make today even better?
_____
_____

Date:

Quote Of The Day

_____

_____

_____

Today I am truly grateful for...

_____

_____

_____

_____

_____

Here's what would make today great...

_____

_____

_____

_____

_____

I am...

_____

_____

_____

Some amazing things that happened today...

_____

_____

Some amazing things that happened today...

_____

_____

What could I have done to make today even better?

_____

_____

Date: _____

Quote Of The Day
_____
_____

Today I am truly grateful for...
_____
_____
_____
_____

Here's what would make today great...
_____
_____
_____
_____

I am...
_____
_____
_____

Some amazing things that happened today...
_____
_____

Some amazing things that happened today...
_____
_____

What could I have done to make today even better?
_____
_____

Date: _____

Quote Of The Day

_____
_____
_____

Today I am truly grateful for...

_____
_____
_____
_____
_____

Here's what would make today great...

_____
_____
_____
_____
_____

I am...

_____
_____
_____

Some amazing things that happened today...

_____
_____

Some amazing things that happened today...

_____
_____
_____

What could I have done to make today even better?

_____
_____

Date: _____

☀

Quote Of The Day
_____
_____
_____

Today I am truly grateful for...
_____
_____
_____
_____
_____

Here's what would make today great...
_____
_____
_____
_____
_____

I am...
_____
_____
_____

Some amazing things that happened today...
_____
_____

Some amazing things that happened today...
_____
_____

What could I have done to make today even better?
_____
_____

Date:

Quote Of The Day

_____
_____
_____

Today I am truly grateful for...

_____
_____
_____
_____
_____

Here's what would make today great...

_____
_____
_____
_____
_____

I am...

_____
_____
_____

Some amazing things that happened today...

_____
_____

Some amazing things that happened today...

_____
_____
_____

What could I have done to make today even better?

_____
_____

ate: _____ ☼

ote Of The Day

_____

_____

day I am truly grateful for...

_____

_____

_____

_____

re's what would make today great...

_____

_____

_____

_____

am...

_____

_____

me amazing things that happened today...

_____

ome amazing things that happened today...

_____

_____

nat could I have done to make today even better?

_____

_____

Date:

Quote Of The Day
_____
- -
_____

Today I am truly grateful for...
- -
_____
- -
_____
- -

Here's what would make today great...
_____
- -
_____
- -
_____

I am...
_____
- -
_____

Some amazing things that happened today...
- -
_____

Some amazing things that happened today...
_____
- -

What could I have done to make today even better?
- -
_____

Date: _____

Quote Of The Day
_____
_____
_____

Today I am truly grateful for...
_____
_____
_____
_____

Here's what would make today great...
_____
_____
_____
_____

I am...
_____
_____
_____

Some amazing things that happened today...
_____
_____

Some amazing things that happened today...
_____
_____

What could I have done to make today even better?
_____
_____

Date: _____

Quote Of The Day
_____
_____
_____

Today I am truly grateful for...
_____
_____
_____
_____
_____

Here's what would make today great...
_____
_____
_____
_____
_____

I am...
_____
_____
_____

Some amazing things that happened today...
_____
_____

Some amazing things that happened today...
_____
_____
_____

What could I have done to make today even better?
_____
_____

ate: _____

☼

uote Of The Day
_____
_____
_____

oday I am truly grateful for...
_____
_____
_____
_____
_____

ere's what would make today great...
_____
_____
_____
_____
_____

am...
_____
_____
_____

ome amazing things that happened today...
_____
_____

ome amazing things that happened today...
_____
_____

hat could I have done to make today even better?
_____
_____

Date:

Quote Of The Day

_____
_____
_____

Today I am truly grateful for...

_____
_____
_____
_____
_____

Here's what would make today great...

_____
_____
_____
_____
_____

I am...

_____
_____
_____

Some amazing things that happened today...

_____
_____

Some amazing things that happened today...

_____
_____

What could I have done to make today even better?

_____
_____

ate: _____

ote Of The Day

_____
_____

day I am truly grateful for...

_____
_____
_____
_____

re's what would make today great...

_____
_____
_____
_____

am...

_____
_____

me amazing things that happened today...

_____

me amazing things that happened today...

_____
_____

nat could I have done to make today even better?

_____
_____

Date:

Quote Of The Day

_____

_____

_____

Today I am truly grateful for...

_____

_____

_____

_____

_____

Here's what would make today great...

_____

_____

_____

_____

_____

I am...

_____

_____

_____

Some amazing things that happened today...

_____

_____

Some amazing things that happened today...

_____

_____

_____

What could I have done to make today even better?

_____

_____

Date: _____

Quote Of The Day

_____

_____

Today I am truly grateful for...

_____

_____

_____

_____

Here's what would make today great...

_____

_____

_____

_____

I am...

_____

_____

Some amazing things that happened today...

_____

Some amazing things that happened today...

_____

What could I have done to make today even better?

_____

Date: _____

Quote Of The Day
_____
_____
_____

Today I am truly grateful for...
_____
_____
_____
_____
_____

Here's what would make today great...
_____
_____
_____
_____
_____

I am...
_____
_____
_____

Some amazing things that happened today...
_____
_____

Some amazing things that happened today...
_____
_____

What could I have done to make today even better?
_____
_____

ate:
_____

Quote Of The Day

_____
_____
_____

Today I am truly grateful for...

_____
_____
_____
_____
_____

Here's what would make today great...

_____
_____
_____
_____
_____

I am...

_____
_____
_____

Some amazing things that happened today...

_____
_____

Some amazing things that happened today...

_____
_____

What could I have done to make today even better?

_____
_____

Date:

Quote Of The Day

_____

_____

_____

Today I am truly grateful for...

_____

_____

_____

_____

_____

Here's what would make today great...

_____

_____

_____

_____

_____

I am...

_____

_____

_____

Some amazing things that happened today...

_____

_____

Some amazing things that happened today...

_____

_____

_____

What could I have done to make today even better?

_____

_____

ate: ☀

ote Of The Day

_____

_____

day I am truly grateful for...

_____

_____

_____

_____

re's what would make today great...

_____

_____

_____

_____

am...

_____

_____

me amazing things that happened today...

_____

_____

ome amazing things that happened today...   ✧ ✧ ☽

_____

_____

nat could I have done to make today even better?

_____

_____

Date:

Quote Of The Day

Today I am truly grateful for...

Here's what would make today great...

I am...

Some amazing things that happened today...

Some amazing things that happened today...

What could I have done to make today even better?

Date: _____

Quote Of The Day

_____
_____

Today I am truly grateful for...

_____
_____
_____
_____

Here's what would make today great...

_____
_____
_____
_____
_____

I am...

_____
_____
_____

Some amazing things that happened today...

_____
_____

Some amazing things that happened today...

_____
_____
_____

What could I have done to make today even better?

_____
_____
_____

Date: _____

Quote Of The Day

_____
_____
_____

Today I am truly grateful for...

_____
_____
_____
_____
_____

Here's what would make today great...

_____
_____
_____
_____
_____

I am...

_____
_____
_____

Some amazing things that happened today...

_____
_____

Some amazing things that happened today...

_____
_____
_____

What could I have done to make today even better?

_____
_____

ate: _____

Quote Of The Day

_____
_____

Today I am truly grateful for...

_____
_____
_____
_____

Here's what would make today great...

_____
_____
_____
_____

I am...

_____
_____

Some amazing things that happened today...

_____
_____

Some amazing things that happened today...

_____
_____

What could I have done to make today even better?

_____
_____

Date: _____

Quote Of The Day

_____
_____
_____

Today I am truly grateful for...

_____
_____
_____
_____
_____

Here's what would make today great...

_____
_____
_____
_____
_____

I am...

_____
_____
_____

Some amazing things that happened today...

_____
_____

Some amazing things that happened today...

_____
_____

What could I have done to make today even better?

_____
_____

Date:

Quote Of The Day

_____

_____

Today I am truly grateful for...

_____

_____

_____

_____

Here's what would make today great...

_____

_____

_____

_____

I am...

_____

_____

Some amazing things that happened today...

_____

Some amazing things that happened today...

_____

What could I have done to make today even better?

_____

_____

Date:

Quote Of The Day

_____

_____

_____

Today I am truly grateful for...

_____

_____

_____

_____

_____

Here's what would make today great...

_____

_____

_____

_____

_____

I am...

_____

_____

_____

Some amazing things that happened today...

_____

_____

Some amazing things that happened today...

_____

_____

_____

What could I have done to make today even better?

_____

_____

Date:

Quote Of The Day

_____
_____

Today I am truly grateful for...

_____
_____
_____
_____

Here's what would make today great...

_____
_____
_____
_____

I am...

_____
_____

Some amazing things that happened today...

_____
_____

Some amazing things that happened today...

_____
_____

What could I have done to make today even better?

_____
_____

Date:

Quote Of The Day

_____

Today I am truly grateful for...

_____

Here's what would make today great...

_____

I am...

_____

Some amazing things that happened today...

_____

Some amazing things that happened today...

_____

What could I have done to make today even better?

_____

Date: ·········· ☀

Quote Of The Day

Today I am truly grateful for...

Here's what would make today great...

I am...

Some amazing things that happened today...

Some amazing things that happened today...

What could I have done to make today even better?

Date:

Quote Of The Day

_____
_____
_____

Today I am truly grateful for...

_____
_____
_____
_____
_____

Here's what would make today great...

_____
_____
_____
_____
_____

I am...

_____
_____
_____

Some amazing things that happened today...

_____
_____

Some amazing things that happened today...

_____
_____
_____

What could I have done to make today even better?

_____
_____

ate: ☀

ote Of The Day

_____

_____

day I am truly grateful for...

_____

_____

_____

_____

re's what would make today great...

_____

_____

_____

_____

am...

_____

_____

me amazing things that happened today...

_____

_____

ome amazing things that happened today...   ✦ ✦ 🌙

_____

nat could I have done to make today even better?

_____

_____

Date:

Quote Of The Day

_____
_____
_____

Today I am truly grateful for...

_____
_____
_____
_____
_____

Here's what would make today great...

_____
_____
_____
_____
_____

I am...

_____
_____
_____

Some amazing things that happened today...

_____
_____

Some amazing things that happened today...

_____
_____
_____

What could I have done to make today even better?

_____
_____

Date: _____

Quote Of The Day

_____

_____

Today I am truly grateful for...

_____

_____

_____

_____

Here's what would make today great...

_____

_____

_____

_____

I am...

_____

_____

Some amazing things that happened today...

_____

Some amazing things that happened today...

_____

What could I have done to make today even better?

_____

_____

Date: ☀

Quote Of The Day

_____

_____

Today I am truly grateful for...

_____

_____

_____

_____

Here's what would make today great...

_____

_____

_____

_____

I am...

_____

_____

Some amazing things that happened today...

_____

Some amazing things that happened today... ✨ ✨ 🌙

_____

_____

What could I have done to make today even better?

_____

_____

ate: _____

☼

uote Of The Day

_____
_____

day I am truly grateful for...

_____
_____
_____
_____
_____

ere's what would make today great...

_____
_____
_____
_____
_____

am...

_____
_____
_____

me amazing things that happened today...

_____
_____

ome amazing things that happened today...

_____

hat could I have done to make today even better?

_____
_____

Date:

Quote Of The Day

_____

_____

Today I am truly grateful for...

_____

_____

_____

_____

Here's what would make today great...

_____

_____

_____

_____

I am...

_____

_____

Some amazing things that happened today...

_____

Some amazing things that happened today...

_____

_____

What could I have done to make today even better?

_____

_____

Date: _____

☀

Quote Of The Day

_____
_____
_____

Today I am truly grateful for...

_____
_____
_____
_____
_____

Here's what would make today great...

_____
_____
_____
_____

I am...

_____
_____
_____

Some amazing things that happened today...

_____
_____

Some amazing things that happened today...

_____
_____

What could I have done to make today even better?

_____
_____

Date:

Quote Of The Day

Today I am truly grateful for...

Here's what would make today great...

I am...

Some amazing things that happened today...

Some amazing things that happened today...

What could I have done to make today even better?

Date: _____

Quote Of The Day
_____
_____

Today I am truly grateful for...
_____
_____
_____
_____

Here's what would make today great...
_____
_____
_____
_____

I am...
_____
_____
_____

Some amazing things that happened today...
_____
_____

Some amazing things that happened today...
_____
_____

What could I have done to make today even better?
_____
_____

Date: _____

☼

Quote Of The Day

_____

_____

_____

Today I am truly grateful for...

_____

_____

_____

_____

_____

Here's what would make today great...

_____

_____

_____

_____

_____

I am...

_____

_____

_____

Some amazing things that happened today...

_____

_____

Some amazing things that happened today...

_____

_____

_____

What could I have done to make today even better?

_____

_____

ate:

Quote Of The Day

_____
_____

Today I am truly grateful for...

_____
_____
_____
_____

Here's what would make today great...

_____
_____
_____
_____

I am...

_____
_____

Some amazing things that happened today...

_____
_____

Some amazing things that happened today...

_____
_____

What could I have done to make today even better?

_____
_____

Date:

Quote Of The Day

Today I am truly grateful for...

Here's what would make today great...

I am...

Some amazing things that happened today...

Some amazing things that happened today...

What could I have done to make today even better?

Date: _____

☀

Quote Of The Day

_____
_____

Today I am truly grateful for...

_____
_____
_____
_____

Here's what would make today great...

_____
_____
_____
_____

I am...

_____
_____

Some amazing things that happened today...

_____
_____

Some amazing things that happened today...

_____
_____

What could I have done to make today even better?

_____
_____

Date:

Quote Of The Day
_____
_____
_____

Today I am truly grateful for...
_____
_____
_____
_____
_____

Here's what would make today great...
_____
_____
_____
_____
_____

I am...
_____
_____
_____

Some amazing things that happened today...
_____
_____

Some amazing things that happened today...
_____
_____

What could I have done to make today even better?
_____
_____

Date: _____

Quote Of The Day

_____

_____

Today I am truly grateful for...

_____

_____

_____

_____

Here's what would make today great...

_____

_____

_____

_____

I am...

_____

_____

_____

Some amazing things that happened today...

_____

_____

Some amazing things that happened today...

_____

_____

_____

What could I have done to make today even better?

_____

_____

Date: _____

☀

Quote Of The Day

_____
_____
_____

Today I am truly grateful for...

_____
_____
_____
_____
_____

Here's what would make today great...

_____
_____
_____
_____
_____

I am...

_____
_____
_____

Some amazing things that happened today...

_____
_____

Some amazing things that happened today...

_____
_____
_____

What could I have done to make today even better?

_____
_____

Date: _____

☀

Quote Of The Day

_____
_____
_____

Today I am truly grateful for...

_____
_____
_____
_____
_____

Here's what would make today great...

_____
_____
_____
_____
_____

I am...

_____
_____
_____
_____

Some amazing things that happened today...

_____
_____

Some amazing things that happened today...

_____
_____

What could I have done to make today even better?

_____
_____

Date:

Quote Of The Day

Today I am truly grateful for...

Here's what would make today great...

I am...

Some amazing things that happened today...

Some amazing things that happened today...

What could I have done to make today even better?

ate: _____

Note Of The Day
_____
_____

Today I am truly grateful for...
_____
_____
_____
_____

Here's what would make today great...
_____
_____
_____
_____

I am...
_____
_____

Some amazing things that happened today...
_____

Some amazing things that happened today...
_____

What could I have done to make today even better?
_____
_____

Date: _____

Quote Of The Day

_____

_____

Today I am truly grateful for...

_____

_____

_____

_____

Here's what would make today great...

_____

_____

_____

_____

I am...

_____

_____

Some amazing things that happened today...

_____

_____

Some amazing things that happened today...

_____

_____

What could I have done to make today even better?

_____

Date: _____

Quote Of The Day

_____

_____

_____

Today I am truly grateful for...

_____

_____

_____

_____

Here's what would make today great...

_____

_____

_____

_____

I am...

_____

_____

Some amazing things that happened today...

_____

Some amazing things that happened today...

_____

_____

What could I have done to make today even better?

_____

_____

Date:

Quote Of The Day

_____

_____

_____

Today I am truly grateful for...

_____

_____

_____

_____

_____

_____

Here's what would make today great...

_____

_____

_____

_____

_____

_____

I am...

_____

_____

_____

Some amazing things that happened today...

_____

_____

Some amazing things that happened today...

_____

_____

What could I have done to make today even better?

_____

_____

Date:

☀

Quote Of The Day
_____
_____

Today I am truly grateful for...
_____
_____
_____
_____

Here's what would make today great...
_____
_____
_____
_____

I am...
_____
_____
_____

Some amazing things that happened today...
_____
_____

Some amazing things that happened today...

☽

_____
_____

What could I have done to make today even better?
_____
_____

Date:

Quote Of The Day
_____
_____

Today I am truly grateful for...
_____
_____
_____
_____

Here's what would make today great...
_____
_____
_____
_____

I am...
_____
_____

Some amazing things that happened today...
_____
_____

Some amazing things that happened today...
_____
_____

What could I have done to make today even better?
_____
_____

Date: _____

Note Of The Day
_____
_____

Today I am truly grateful for...
_____
_____
_____
_____

Here's what would make today great...
_____
_____
_____
_____

I am...
_____
_____

Some amazing things that happened today...
_____

Some amazing things that happened today...
_____

What could I have done to make today even better?
_____
_____

Date:

Quote Of The Day

_____

_____

Today I am truly grateful for...

_____

_____

_____

_____

Here's what would make today great...

_____

_____

_____

_____

I am...

_____

_____

Some amazing things that happened today...

_____

_____

Some amazing things that happened today...

_____

_____

What could I have done to make today even better?

_____

_____

Date:

Quote Of The Day
_____
_____
_____

Today I am truly grateful for...
_____
_____
_____
_____
_____

Here's what would make today great...
_____
_____
_____
_____
_____

I am...
_____
_____
_____

Some amazing things that happened today...
_____
_____

Some amazing things that happened today...
_____
_____

What could I have done to make today even better?
_____
_____

Date: ☀

Quote Of The Day

_____

_____

Today I am truly grateful for...

_____

_____

_____

_____

Here's what would make today great...

_____

_____

_____

_____

I am...

_____

_____

Some amazing things that happened today...

_____

Some amazing things that happened today...   ✨ ✨ 🌙

_____

_____

What could I have done to make today even better?

_____

_____

Date: _____

☼

Quote Of The Day

_____
_____

Today I am truly grateful for...

_____
_____
_____
_____

Here's what would make today great...

_____
_____
_____
_____

I am...

_____
_____
_____

Some amazing things that happened today...

_____
_____

Some amazing things that happened today...

_____
_____

What could I have done to make today even better?

_____
_____

Date: _____

Quote Of The Day

_____

_____

Today I am truly grateful for...

_____

_____

_____

_____

Here's what would make today great...

_____

_____

_____

_____

I am...

_____

_____

Some amazing things that happened today...

_____

_____

Some amazing things that happened today...

_____

_____

What could I have done to make today even better?

_____

_____

Date:

☀

Quote Of The Day
_____
_____

Today I am truly grateful for...
_____
_____
_____
_____

Here's what would make today great...
_____
_____
_____
_____

I am...
_____
_____
_____

Some amazing things that happened today...
_____
_____

Some amazing things that happened today...
_____
_____

What could I have done to make today even better?
_____
_____

Date:

Quote Of The Day

_____

_____

Today I am truly grateful for...

_____

_____

_____

_____

Here's what would make today great...

_____

_____

_____

_____

I am...

_____

_____

Some amazing things that happened today...

_____

Some amazing things that happened today...

_____

_____

What could I have done to make today even better?

_____

_____

Date: _____

Quote Of The Day
_____
_____

Today I am truly grateful for...
_____
_____
_____
_____
_____

Here's what would make today great...
_____
_____
_____
_____
_____

I am...
_____
_____
_____

Some amazing things that happened today...
_____
_____

Some amazing things that happened today...
_____
_____
_____

What could I have done to make today even better?
_____

Date: _____

Quote Of The Day

_____

_____

Today I am truly grateful for...

_____

_____

_____

_____

Here's what would make today great...

_____

_____

_____

_____

I am...

_____

_____

Some amazing things that happened today...

_____

_____

Some amazing things that happened today...

_____

_____

What could I have done to make today even better?

_____

_____

Date: _____

☀

Quote Of The Day
_____
_____

Today I am truly grateful for...
_____
_____
_____
_____

Here's what would make today great...
_____
_____
_____
_____

I am...
_____
_____
_____

Some amazing things that happened today...
_____
_____

Some amazing things that happened today...
_____
_____

What could I have done to make today even better?
_____
_____

Date:

Quote Of The Day

Today I am truly grateful for...

Here's what would make today great...

I am...

Some amazing things that happened today...

Some amazing things that happened today...

What could I have done to make today even better?

ate: _____

Note Of The Day
_____
_____

Today I am truly grateful for...
_____
_____
_____
_____
_____

Here's what would make today great...
_____
_____
_____
_____
_____

I am...
_____
_____
_____

Some amazing things that happened today...
_____
_____

Some amazing things that happened today...
_____
_____

What could I have done to make today even better?
_____
_____

Date:

Quote Of The Day

_____

_____

Today I am truly grateful for...

_____

_____

_____

_____

Here's what would make today great...

_____

_____

_____

_____

I am...

_____

_____

Some amazing things that happened today...

_____

Some amazing things that happened today...

_____

_____

What could I have done to make today even better?

_____

Date:

Quote Of The Day
_____
_____
_____

Today I am truly grateful for...
_____
_____
_____
_____
_____

Here's what would make today great...
_____
_____
_____
_____
_____

I am...
_____
_____
_____

Some amazing things that happened today...
_____
_____

Some amazing things that happened today...
_____
_____

What could I have done to make today even better?
_____
_____

Date: _____

Quote Of The Day

_____

_____

_____

Today I am truly grateful for...

_____

_____

_____

_____

_____

Here's what would make today great...

_____

_____

_____

_____

_____

I am...

_____

_____

_____

Some amazing things that happened today...

_____

_____

Some amazing things that happened today...

_____

_____

What could I have done to make today even better?

_____

_____

ate: _____

☀

ıote Of The Day
_____
_____

ɔday I am truly grateful for...
_____
_____
_____
_____

ɛre's what would make today great...
_____
_____
_____
_____

am...
_____
_____

ɔme amazing things that happened today...
_____
_____

ɔme amazing things that happened today...
_____
_____

ɦat could I have done to make today even better?
_____
_____

Date:

Quote Of The Day

_____
_____
_____

Today I am truly grateful for...

_____
_____
_____
_____
_____

Here's what would make today great...

_____
_____
_____
_____
_____

I am...

_____
_____
_____

Some amazing things that happened today...

_____
_____
_____

Some amazing things that happened today...

_____
_____
_____

What could I have done to make today even better?

_____
_____

Date: _____

☀

Note Of The Day

_____
_____
_____

Today I am truly grateful for...

_____
_____
_____
_____
_____

Here's what would make today great...

_____
_____
_____
_____
_____

I am...

_____
_____
_____

Some amazing things that happened today...

_____
_____

Some amazing things that happened today...   ✦ ✦ ☽

_____
_____

What could I have done to make today even better?

_____
_____

Date: _____

Quote Of The Day

_____
_____
_____

Today I am truly grateful for...

_____
_____
_____
_____
_____

Here's what would make today great...

_____
_____
_____
_____
_____

I am...

_____
_____
_____

Some amazing things that happened today...

_____
_____

Some amazing things that happened today...

_____
_____
_____

What could I have done to make today even better?

_____
_____

Date: _____

Quote Of The Day
_____
_____

Today I am truly grateful for...
_____
_____
_____
_____

Here's what would make today great...
_____
_____
_____
_____

I am...
_____
_____

Some amazing things that happened today...
_____
_____

Some amazing things that happened today...
_____
_____

What could I have done to make today even better?
_____
_____

Date:

☀

Quote Of The Day

_____

_____

Today I am truly grateful for...

_____

_____

_____

_____

Here's what would make today great...

_____

_____

_____

_____

I am...

_____

_____

Some amazing things that happened today...

_____

_____

Some amazing things that happened today...

_____

_____

What could I have done to make today even better?

_____

_____

ate: _____

Quote Of The Day

_____
_____
_____

Today I am truly grateful for...

_____
_____
_____
_____
_____

Here's what would make today great...

_____
_____
_____
_____
_____

I am...

_____
_____
_____

Some amazing things that happened today...

_____
_____

Some amazing things that happened today...

_____
_____

What could I have done to make today even better?

_____
_____

Date: _____

Quote Of The Day

_____
_____
_____

Today I am truly grateful for...

_____
_____
_____
_____
_____

Here's what would make today great...

_____
_____
_____
_____
_____

I am...

_____
_____
_____

Some amazing things that happened today...

_____
_____

Some amazing things that happened today...

_____
_____

What could I have done to make today even better?

_____
_____

ate:

Note Of The Day

_____

_____

day I am truly grateful for...

_____

_____

_____

_____

re's what would make today great...

_____

_____

_____

_____

am...

_____

_____

me amazing things that happened today...

_____

ome amazing things that happened today...

_____

_____

hat could I have done to make today even better?

_____

_____

Date:

Quote Of The Day

_____

_____

_____

Today I am truly grateful for...

_____

_____

_____

_____

_____

Here's what would make today great...

_____

_____

_____

_____

_____

I am...

_____

_____

_____

Some amazing things that happened today...

_____

_____

Some amazing things that happened today...

_____

_____

_____

What could I have done to make today even better?

_____

_____

Date: _____

Quote Of The Day

_____

_____

Today I am truly grateful for...

_____

_____

_____

_____

Here's what would make today great...

_____

_____

_____

_____

I am...

_____

_____

Some amazing things that happened today...

_____

_____

Some amazing things that happened today...

_____

_____

What could I have done to make today even better?

_____

_____

Date: _____

☀

Quote Of The Day

_____
_____
_____

Today I am truly grateful for...

_____
_____
_____
_____
_____

Here's what would make today great...

_____
_____
_____
_____
_____

I am...

_____
_____
_____

Some amazing things that happened today...

_____
_____

Some amazing things that happened today...

_____
_____

What could I have done to make today even better?

_____
_____

ate: ☀

ote Of The Day

_____
_____

day I am truly grateful for...

_____
_____
_____
_____

re's what would make today great...

_____
_____
_____
_____

am...

_____
_____
_____

me amazing things that happened today...

_____
_____

ome amazing things that happened today... ✨ ✨ 🌙

_____
_____

hat could I have done to make today even better?

_____
_____

Date: _____

Quote Of The Day
_____
_____
_____

Today I am truly grateful for...
_____
_____
_____
_____
_____

Here's what would make today great...
_____
_____
_____
_____
_____

I am...
_____
_____
_____

Some amazing things that happened today...
_____
_____

Some amazing things that happened today...
_____
_____

What could I have done to make today even better?
_____
_____

ate: ☀

ote Of The Day
_____
_____

day I am truly grateful for...
_____
_____
_____
_____

re's what would make today great...
_____
_____
_____
_____

am...
_____
_____

me amazing things that happened today...
_____

ome amazing things that happened today...   ✦ ✦ ☽
_____
_____

nat could I have done to make today even better?
_____
_____

Date:

Quote Of The Day

_____

_____

_____

Today I am truly grateful for...

_____

_____

_____

_____

_____

Here's what would make today great...

_____

_____

_____

_____

_____

I am...

_____

_____

_____

Some amazing things that happened today...

_____

_____

Some amazing things that happened today...

_____

_____

_____

What could I have done to make today even better?

_____

_____

Date:

Quote Of The Day
_____
_____

Today I am truly grateful for...
_____
_____
_____
_____

Here's what would make today great...
_____
_____
_____
_____

I am...
_____
_____

Some amazing things that happened today...
_____
_____

Some amazing things that happened today...
_____
_____

What could I have done to make today even better?
_____
_____

Date: _____   ☀

Quote Of The Day
_____
_____

Today I am truly grateful for...
_____
_____
_____
_____

Here's what would make today great...
_____
_____
_____
_____

I am...
_____
_____

Some amazing things that happened today...
_____

Some amazing things that happened today...   ✨ ✨ ✨🌙
_____
_____

What could I have done to make today even better?
_____
_____

Date: ☀

Quote Of The Day
_____
_____

Today I am truly grateful for...
_____
_____
_____
_____

Here's what would make today great...
_____
_____
_____
_____
_____

I am...
_____
_____

Some amazing things that happened today...
_____
_____

Some amazing things that happened today...   ✦ ✦ 🌙
_____
_____

What could I have done to make today even better?
_____
_____

Date: _____

Quote Of The Day

_____
_____

Today I am truly grateful for...

_____
_____
_____
_____

Here's what would make today great...

_____
_____
_____
_____

I am...

_____
_____

Some amazing things that happened today...

_____
_____

Some amazing things that happened today...

_____
_____

What could I have done to make today even better?

_____
_____

ate: ☀

ote Of The Day

_____
_____

day I am truly grateful for...

_____
_____
_____
_____

re's what would make today great...

_____
_____
_____
_____

am...

_____
_____

me amazing things that happened today...

_____

me amazing things that happened today...

_____

at could I have done to make today even better?

_____

Date:

Quote Of The Day

_____

_____

_____

Today I am truly grateful for...

_____

_____

_____

_____

_____

Here's what would make today great...

_____

_____

_____

_____

_____

I am...

_____

_____

_____

Some amazing things that happened today...

_____

_____

Some amazing things that happened today...

_____

_____

What could I have done to make today even better?

_____

_____

Date:

Quote Of The Day

_____
_____
_____

Today I am truly grateful for...

_____
_____
_____
_____
_____

Here's what would make today great...

_____
_____
_____
_____
_____

I am...

_____
_____
_____

Some amazing things that happened today...

_____

Some amazing things that happened today...

_____
_____

What could I have done to make today even better?

_____

Date: _____

Quote Of The Day

_____
_____
_____

Today I am truly grateful for...

_____
_____
_____
_____
_____

Here's what would make today great...

_____
_____
_____
_____
_____

I am...

_____
_____
_____

Some amazing things that happened today...

_____
_____

Some amazing things that happened today...

_____
_____
_____

What could I have done to make today even better?

_____
_____

Date:

Note Of The Day
_____
_____
_____

Today I am truly grateful for...
_____
_____
_____
_____
_____
_____

Here's what would make today great...
_____
_____
_____
_____
_____

I am...
_____
_____
_____

Some amazing things that happened today...
_____
_____

Some amazing things that happened today...
_____
_____

What could I have done to make today even better?
_____
_____

Date:

Quote Of The Day
_____
_____
_____

Today I am truly grateful for...
_____
_____
_____
_____
_____

Here's what would make today great...
_____
_____
_____
_____
_____

I am...
_____
_____
_____

Some amazing things that happened today...
_____
_____

Some amazing things that happened today...
_____
_____
_____

What could I have done to make today even better?
_____
_____

ate: _____

Note Of The Day

_____
_____

Today I am truly grateful for...

_____
_____
_____
_____

Here's what would make today great...

_____
_____
_____
_____

I am...

_____
_____

Some amazing things that happened today...

_____
_____

Some amazing things that happened today...

_____
_____

What could I have done to make today even better?

_____
_____

Date:

Quote Of The Day

_____
_____
_____

Today I am truly grateful for...

_____
_____
_____
_____
_____

Here's what would make today great...

_____
_____
_____
_____
_____

I am...

_____
_____
_____

Some amazing things that happened today...

_____
_____

Some amazing things that happened today...

_____
_____

What could I have done to make today even better?

_____
_____

Date: _____

Quote Of The Day

_____
_____
_____

Today I am truly grateful for...

_____
_____
_____
_____
_____

Here's what would make today great...

_____
_____
_____
_____
_____

I am...

_____
_____
_____

Some amazing things that happened today...

_____
_____

Some amazing things that happened today...

_____
_____
_____

What could I have done to make today even better?

_____
_____

Date: _____

Quote Of The Day

_____

_____

_____

Today I am truly grateful for...

_____

_____

_____

_____

_____

Here's what would make today great...

_____

_____

_____

_____

_____

I am...

_____

_____

_____

Some amazing things that happened today...

_____

_____

Some amazing things that happened today...

_____

_____

_____

What could I have done to make today even better?

_____

_____

Date: ☀

Quote Of The Day

_____

_____

_____

Today I am truly grateful for...

_____

_____

_____

_____

Here's what would make today great...

_____

_____

_____

_____

_____

I am...

_____

_____

_____

Some amazing things that happened today...

_____

_____

Some amazing things that happened today... ✧ ✧ 🌙

_____

_____

What could I have done to make today even better?

_____

_____

Date: _____

Quote Of The Day

_____

_____

_____

Today I am truly grateful for...

_____

_____

_____

_____

_____

Here's what would make today great...

_____

_____

_____

_____

_____

I am...

_____

_____

_____

Some amazing things that happened today...

_____

_____

Some amazing things that happened today...

_____

_____

_____

What could I have done to make today even better?

_____

_____

ate: _____ ☀

Note Of The Day
_____
_____

Today I am truly grateful for...
_____
_____
_____
_____

Here's what would make today great...
_____
_____
_____
_____
_____

I am...
_____
_____
_____

Some amazing things that happened today...
_____
_____

Some amazing things that happened today... ✨ ✨ 🌙
_____
_____

What could I have done to make today even better?
_____
_____

Date:

Quote Of The Day

_____
_____

Today I am truly grateful for...

_____
_____
_____
_____

Here's what would make today great...

_____
_____
_____
_____

I am...

_____
_____

Some amazing things that happened today...

_____
_____

Some amazing things that happened today...

_____
_____

What could I have done to make today even better?

_____

Date: _____

Quote Of The Day

_____
_____
_____

Today I am truly grateful for...

_____
_____
_____
_____

Here's what would make today great...

_____
_____
_____
_____

I am...

_____
_____

Some amazing things that happened today...

_____
_____

Some amazing things that happened today...

_____
_____

What could I have done to make today even better?

_____
_____

Date: _____

Quote Of The Day

_____
_____

Today I am truly grateful for...

_____
_____
_____
_____
_____

Here's what would make today great...

_____
_____
_____
_____
_____

I am...

_____
_____
_____

Some amazing things that happened today...

_____
_____

Some amazing things that happened today...

_____
_____
_____

What could I have done to make today even better?

_____
_____

Date:

☀

Quote Of The Day
_____
_____

Today I am truly grateful for...
_____
_____
_____
_____

Here's what would make today great...
_____
_____
_____
_____

I am...
_____
_____
_____

Some amazing things that happened today...
_____
_____

Some amazing things that happened today...

☽

_____
_____

What could I have done to make today even better?
_____
_____

Date:

Quote Of The Day

_____

_____

Today I am truly grateful for...

_____

_____

_____

_____

Here's what would make today great...

_____

_____

_____

_____

I am...

_____

_____

Some amazing things that happened today...

_____

_____

Some amazing things that happened today...

_____

_____

What could I have done to make today even better?

_____

_____

Printed in Great Britain
by Amazon

56204820R00088